MW01122303

Joan
Parsons
Kuraitis ♡

Simpatico
A Collection of Love Letters to My Mother

Joan Parsons Kuraitis

Orange Hat Publishing
www.orangehatpublishing.com - Waukesha, WI

For information, please contact:

Orange Hat Publishing
www.orangehatpublishing.com
info@orangehatpublishing.com

Cover photographs by Nicolle Grassl

The author has made every effort to ensure that the accuracy of the information within this book was correct at time of publication. The author does not assume and hereby disclaims any liability to any party for any loss, damage, or disruption caused by errors or omissions, whether such errors or omissions result from accident, negligence, or any other cause.

Printed in the United States of America

www.orangehatpublishing.com

For my mother, Florence Gable Parsons, who paved the highway of mothering for me by revealing her strengths and wisdom, all gained through years of experience.

For my daughters Kristina Kuraitis Kennedy and Anne Kuraitis Aubry, who patiently allowed me to practice my Mommy skills on them.

"All that I am, or ever hope to be, I owe to my angel mother."

Abraham Lincoln

Prologue

Several years ago, I found myself drawn to the writing art form known as the memoir. Those that spoke to me in a profound way included anything by Jen Lancaster for her wit and humor, along with her ability to stand up straight again after a fall. Also on my list of notable memoirs is *Eat, Pray, Love* by Elizabeth Gilbert for the way the author rebuilt her life during a year of travel and prayer. In addition to those favorites I would include *My Life in France* by Julia Child which clearly illustrates that each of us has the capacity to develop the tiniest seed of an idea such as teaching French cooking to American women into a thriving culinary empire.

Digesting the lives of ordinary women, often at critical junctures in their life journey, made me focus on my own mother in a deeper way. My mother's turning points became apparent to me in my early teens. If the heroines of my favorite stories were able to deliver positive outcomes as a result of their struggles, then certainly the stories of my own dear mother and her life challenges could provide an uplifting message of love, friendship, and hope.

Florence Gable Parsons lived to be exactly sixty-two and a half years of age, a short life by today's standards. She was a beloved daughter, sister, friend, wife, mother, and grandmother. What made her life especially memorable to me was the gracious and poised way she carried herself through life while experiencing both triumph and tragedy such as the much-too-early death of her mother, the sudden remarriage of her father, and the loss of her one true love. This loving collection of letters is my way of documenting her life, and our special bond as mother and daughter. From my teen years forward she always reminded me that we were *simpatico*, Mom's way of referring to our relationship as more like two peas in a pod.

Now, nearly thirty years since her death, this collection of love letters outlines the story of her life and our unique relationship, as well as our kindred spirits. These stories illustrate and honor her mothering style, and acknowledge her many pearls of wisdom I absorbed both by observation and conversation. A few of my mother's lessons live on in my daughters whenever I witness them dressing in simple classic clothing, writing thoughtful thank you notes, and drilling the rules of etiquette into the hearts and minds of their young children.

Being without her here on Earth has never weakened the strength of our relationship, but enhanced it in many ways. Each and every letter serves as a tribute to my enduring devotion to the only woman I will ever call Mom.

Joan Parsons Kuraitis
January, 2017

1950's

Notes for the Reader

Throughout the decade of the 1950's, I was a baby, toddler, and child. These letters are written to reflect the innocence of the time, the place, and the relationships of the people around me. This section is also meant to lay the groundwork for letters that follow, and I use a more mature voice to describe locations, feelings and emotions, my neighborhood, friends, and school.

As a reader, consume these stories with childlike wonder, but appreciate them in a way that reflects your own understanding and knowledge of families. As the decades continue, the letters and their contents will surely reflect the voice of an adolescent (1960's) and young adult (1970's) and will grow as I have grown over the years.

Please read with an open heart. Every letter is presented with love as a way of documenting and describing my mother's life, as well as the people, places, and activities that impacted her journey as a young wife, mother, and friend.

January 1, 1952

Dear Mom,

How are you feeling? You are approaching the end of your second trimester with your third pregnancy. Already, you have been blessed with two baby girls--Virginia Gable born in 1945, and Georgia Ann making her appearance in 1948. You may be hoping for a boy this time. With a due date about twelve weeks away, there is time to wonder about and plan for this new little life.

Today, you probably prepared three meals, did some laundry, and put away the Christmas decorations. This is your habit to wait until New Year's Day to remove the holiday decor from the living room, as well as the real-life evergreen tree with colored bulb lights and brilliant glass ornaments. Always, there is a soft white angel at the top of the tree. Everything is carefully wrapped in tissue paper, to be unpacked next year in a flurry of activity on Christmas Eve after your children fall asleep. You and Dad work very hard to create Christmas morning magic with lights that flicker off ornaments, gift wrap, and toys.

The house you reside in is located at 3503 Fort Roberdeau Avenue in Altoona, Pennsylvania, a charming two story brick and frame dwelling with a one-car attached garage. Gleaming hardwood floors are front and center in every room. This is the city of your birth and you seem happy to call Altoona with its seventy-seven thousand residents home.

Directly across the street is the home of George and Clarimae Good, better known as "Pete" to family and friends. Pete is also expecting a baby in the spring, but this will be her fourth child after Carol, Lynn, and George. Although you and Pete are two very tired mothers, there is the potential for a new friendship and pairing, once again, when these new little babies grow up to be playmates and best friends.

Today is a new beginning since it is the first day of 1952. My hope for you is that your remaining weeks of pregnancy are comfortable, and

4

healthy, with a short labor and delivery.
I love you very much.

Joanie

April 15, 1952

Dear Mom,

Very early on this Tuesday morning, just past midnight, you delivered me at Altoona Hospital. I am your third daughter, and you named me Joan Kantner Parsons. You knew in your heart of hearts that Dad, William Kantner Parsons, your husband, was desperate to have a son, so my name copied his. Word of a third daughter played out in the wee hours of the hospital waiting area precisely in the following manner. When Dad heard the news from the doctor in the fathers' lounge, his reply was expressed this way: "Are you sure? Look again."

Your third baby girl was a good sleeper and didn't fuss much. Sometime later you said: "Joanie, if I hadn't had you, I wouldn't have known what a good baby was." That statement spoke volumes to me about your work load with Gingy, a fussy baby, and Georgia, a difficult sleeper. My big sisters were a handful for any parent, experienced or not.

The second floor nursery where you brought me home was actually referred to as "the baby room." It was tiny by today's standards, only about eight feet by ten feet, with two small windows, one facing the back yard, and the other overlooking our side yard. The room was positioned just next to the master bedroom. From my first recollections of "the baby room" as a toddler, it had pale pink walls, hardwood flooring, and an older area rug, something acquired second hand from Grandpa and Grandma Gable, with deep red cabbage roses. Also present were two narrow closets which made for a very neat and cozy room of my own.

Although the birth of a third daughter was not Dad's first choice, you loved me unconditionally. Years later, I came to realize that Dad's ideal family consisted of a father, mother, and four children (two boys and two girls), just like his own family of origin. For you, though, the most desirable family consisted of a father, mother, and just two children (both girls) as in your nuclear family. My birth was something of a compromise for both you and Dad. Thank you for carrying me for nine months, then delivering me safely to the catching hands of Dr. Hull.

I love you so much.

Joanie

December 25, 1952

Dear Mom,

This is my first Christmas. Today, you are a lovely twenty-eight year old wife, mother, friend, neighbor, daughter, and home owner. Your life is full, but you smile patiently as you juggle each role.

On this Christmas morning, 1952, I was eight months old, and oh, so chubby. My round face, bald head, and wide ears were adorable, although no hint of a smile played on my face. With all the celebrating, I certainly did appear content and engaged. A soft faint dusting of dark baby fine hair filled my round head. My eyes sparkled bright hazel, just like yours.

Gingy and Georgia, both received fancy new wooden sleds for Christmas with their names painted in red block letters on each. For our "sisters" photo, I was positioned between each sibling for the shot while sitting atop one of the shiny new sleds. Since I didn't receive a sled of my own, most likely I will share with my sisters in years to come. Georgia seemed elated by the expression on her face, and Gingy was genuinely happy as she smiled for the camera.

This year, as in years past, we enjoyed a delicious Christmas dinner of turkey and all the trimmings at the Gable home later in the day. Your parents lived just a brief walking distance from our Fort Roberdeau home, and also in the Mansion Park district of Altoona. In fact, Grandma and Grandpa Gable resided just a few doors down from Baker Mansion where all the neighborhood kids enjoyed the best double decker sledding hill in the area.

Christmas is truly a magical day, and this year began the tradition of many holiday celebrations for me as your baby girl.

I love you very much.

Joanie

1953

Dear Mom,

This year I turn one. My cheeks are rosy, and my disposition pleasant each day. I continue to be a very good sleeper. With bona fide elephant ears, you must remain diligent about turning my ears flat for nap time so they won't grow even wider. Without this attention to detail, I might take flight and soar through the air just as Dumbo did in the Disney film by the same name.

Still my hair is nothing more than a fuzzy crown of dark wisps. My eyes are inquisitive and thoughtful. I seem to be a bouncy, round, and good natured baby. My favorite word is "Ma-Ma" which probably plays like a broken record in your head all day.

Gingy attends grade school full time, and Georgia plays at home all day as a preschooler. Our mornings are spent in the play room with its Dutch door and high piles of stuffed toys. The space reminds everyone of an oversized play pen. There are hardwood floors throughout the house and the play room is no exception. The room streams with sunlight each morning. That contained and safe space allows you to do some home keeping while Georgia and I play among the toys.

In 1953, our milk arrived at the back door twice a week (Tuesday and Saturday) courtesy of a delivery man from Logan Bell Farms. At that time, we all drank whole milk. Also readily available in our community was an egg man, actually a local farmer, who knocked on the back door once a week to deliver fresh eggs from his basket. That lifestyle was typical of middle-class America in the 1950's.

I was surrounded by family and friends including maternal grandparents George and Florence Gable, as well as paternal grandparents, Chester and Helen Parsons. Grandpa Gable was the President of Gable's Department Store in Altoona, and Grandma Gable, a full-time homemaker, was highly skilled in cooking, baking, sewing, and quilt making. Grandpa Parsons was the founder of Parsons Agency in Altoona, selling real estate and insurance to the locals, while Grandma Parsons stayed home and cooked and cleaned with enthusiasm.

I hope you are enjoying your life as a young wife and mother. A daily routine of chores and child care must be tedious. Yet, you never seem to complain.

I love you with all my heart.

Joanie

July 1, 1954

Dear Mom,

What was special about today--Thursday, July 1st? I found a lovely black and white photo of you and twelve other ladies looking oh, so fine, on that warm summer afternoon at Aunt Louise Parsons' house. Aunt Louise, appearing quite elegant in her form fitting sleeveless white linen dress, along with you and Aunt Helen Basler, stood together in the front row of the picture, taken on the porch of Aunt Louise's home at 408 Ruskin Drive. The white picket fence added the charm of 1950's Americana to the neat two-story house, along with the outdoor mailbox attached near the front door.

Mom, you appeared slim and radiant in your dark plaid shirtwaist dress and earrings, bracelet, and rings. Clearly, I learned my love of accessorizing from you at a young age, just by watching you dress for an event. Your hair was cut short in the popular bob to just over the ears, and you sported short bangs. I loved this look on you. It mirrored the image of First Lady Mamie Eisenhower, married to your beloved thirty-fourth United States President, Dwight D. Eisenhower, former World War II General and revered war hero.

That afternoon captured a moment in time and showed me the mommy I knew and loved from the 1950's, smiling with friends and in-laws who lived in the area. You, Louise, and Helen made a charming, stylish, and witty trio of well read and interesting ladies. I would *love* to have been a fly on the wall at your monthly Bridge Club meetings, afternoon tea dates with Pete Good, and evening house parties when laughter erupted over stories and jokes.

I hope to be just like you someday.
With love,

Joanie

October 28, 1954

Dear Mom,

Today--Thursday, October 28th--you turn thirty years old. Your life revolves around taking care of others: your three little girls and your success oriented husband who is both a high achieving business owner and competitive badminton and tennis enthusiast. Life in Altoona, Pennsylvania, is very different from the world of New York City, and *Life Magazine*, where your baby sister, Virginia Gable (A.K.A "Boonie"), lives and works. Do you miss glamorous parties, dressing "to the nines," and sipping champagne?

On a regular basis, I have observed the long afternoon telephone conversations you enjoyed with Boonie, while perched on the corner of the desk in the living room. You have a tendency to gaze longingly in the mirror that hangs above the desk while engaged in deep sisterly conversations. What did you siblings discuss? Was it work and boyfriends for the single Boonie, or the latest developmental milestones for Gingy, Georgia, and me? I never really did hear the discussion, just noticed your smiling face as you conversed with Boonie.

I imagined life for you was daily childcare, housework, and cooking with Gingy at age nine, Georgia who was six, and me at just two and a half. Did you know that while you were back in bed for a morning nap, I watched *Captain Kangaroo* on our black and white television, and smeared Skippy Peanut Butter all over my hands? I have observed you carefully as you lathered your own hands with Ponds Cold Cream to keep them smooth and soft. Skippy seemed like hand cream to me. You never noticed the missing peanut butter and my hands were washed clean by me when you appeared from your morning nap. All of this happened while the house was quiet and Dad was off to work as a partner in Parsons Agency selling real estate, and Gingy and Georgia were tucked away safely in aging classrooms at Baker School on Ward Avenue.

Surely, this birthday is special to you. You are still my glamorous mother, even in an apron. However, there is a part of me that wonders if you long for the days, and years from 1942 to 1944, spent in New York City while you were a student at Edgewood Park, the finishing school for girls, and dating Dad, a young Naval officer? Perhaps you do, based on the way you hang onto each and every word of Boonie's stories delivered by phone.

Promise me you won't change.

I love you very much.

Joanie

1955

Dear Mom,

This year I turn three years old. For the first time, I am part of the summer vacation to the Jersey Shore with you, Dad, Gingy, and Georgia, as well as Grandma and Grandpa Gable. The Gables always rent a spacious house on the beach for one full month each and every summer. Up until this summer, I was home with Mimi and Clark Holton, my beloved second parents. As empty nesters, the Holtons happily provided care and nurturing as my sitters whenever there was a need for their services.

The Jersey Shore was a fascinating place to explore, splash, run, and create a variety of sand sculptures. The first week was the most challenging--frolicking in the waves of the Atlantic Ocean while preventing a blistering sunburn. Scorched skin was part of the deal at the Shore. Along with the red sore blisters came globs of cool soothing Noxema, rubbed gently into my nose, shoulders, and back each night at bedtime.

My favorite part of the nightly routine was the ice cream truck that made its rounds after dark each evening. Such a treat to be able to stay up late until 9 p.m. and enjoy an ice cold cherry popsicle before turning in after a long and active day at the beach.

Every morning at daybreak, I awakened and, on tiptoes, made my way to the large living room. I spotted Grandma Gable sitting in a rocking chair and gazing out the picture window toward the vast Atlantic Ocean with its soothing rhythmic waves. With a silent house and the gentle waves just outside the door, Grandma and I bonded over quiet conversation at the start of each day while she softly rocked, and I sat at her feet on the floor.

Another daily ritual I especially enjoyed back at home as a three-year-old was watching *Captain Kangaroo* on our black and white Philco television set in the play room. The Captain had many friends on the show including Mr. Green Jeans, Bunny Rabbit, Mr. Moose, and Grandfather Clock. The Captain's soothing voice and quiet demeanor captivated my attention as he welcomed friends and guests to his show every day.

After Dad left for work, and Gingy and Georgia were occupied at Baker School for the day, you tucked yourself back in bed to catch up with your sleep. Downstairs, I had the freedom to roam the house on my own for a few hours while playing, watching television, and enjoying the pleasures of a peanut butter hand massage.

This year felt like a warm comforting hug in the form of a peaceful and predictable daily routine. How would my life unfold over the next few years? Only time would tell. For now, thank you for creating a nurturing environment with plenty of hours of independent exploration and a regular routine for meals, play, and bedtime.

I love you, Mommy.

Joanie

1956

Dear Mom,

This year I am four, and you are a beautiful and youthful Mommy of thirty-two. Waggie Good and I are best friends, and we have started morning kindergarten at Mrs. Hoffman's private school in a church basement, five days a week. Waggie, the across-the-street neighbor, is a blue-eyed blond-haired cutie with energy to burn. His curious and outgoing personality is the yin to my yang which is quiet and reserved.

I adored Mrs. Hoffman and the kindergarten routine each morning. Daddy drove both Waggie and me to school, just like big kids. We enjoyed a schedule of coloring, singing songs, and learning to read the hands of a clock. I was especially good at the time- telling skill. In fact, I could beat the other students in a competition Mrs. Hoffman set up for us which made me feel very special. My mornings flew by in the blink of an eye.

Waggie's Mommy, Pete, picked us up at school close to lunchtime, and we rode home together in the back seat of her car. She pulled into her driveway and I ran across the street to our house where you were waiting by the door.

One afternoon, after lunch, I was without my best friend. He had to take a nap. I was minding my own business in the back of Waggie's house as I pulled a loose piece of mortar in and out of the chimney. My thoughts wondered someplace else as I sang out loud "Who's Afraid of the Big Bad Wolf?". And, then I turned around. There, staring at me was THE big bad wolf, so close, I could see his huge dark eyes fixed on me.

That's when I took off, ran home, just across the street, and flew in the front screen door. You sat calmly and quietly on the living room couch reading. When I explained to you that I had witnessed the big bad wolf from the "Red Riding Hood" story I loved to hear at bedtime, you casually replied, "Oh, that's just Sheba, the Couples' dog". Still, that explanation didn't exactly calm my fears. Knowing that Mr. and Mrs. Couples' dog, Sheba, was free to roam the neighborhood panicked me and made my heart beat faster and faster.

Now, at the age of four, I am afraid of dogs, large and small. Mommy, dogs really do scare me. I stop dead in my tracks and quiver whenever I spot a dog in the neighborhood regardless of the size. This is a serious fear for me, yet you seem so calm.

Thank you for trying to make a fully-grown black German Shepard seem like a harmless puppy.

I still love you so very much.

Joanie

1957

Dear Mom,

You and I both know how this scar on the right side of my forehead appeared. You were just as annoyed with Georgia as I was the afternoon she shoved me hard into the corner of the living room coffee table.

On a quiet afternoon while you puttered in the kitchen, Georgia and I were on the living room couch singing songs. I stood up to leave the room and within an instant Georgia pushed me out of her way. Unfortunately, my head became the flying object and landed on the ninety-degree edge (no rounded corners to soften the blow) of our wooden coffee table.

The immediate screams and wailing along with gushing squirts of blood drew you instantly from the kitchen to assess the situation. Upon seeing your youngest child cupping a handful of blood, you dialed Dad's office number from the desk phone with the most panicked of expressions and a look that revealed your own fear. Dad advised you to call Dr. Dick Magee, a family friend, and try to see him immediately. You did, and soon we were loaded into the car and on our way to Dr. Magee's office, a brief ten- minute drive.

I held a fancy guest towel to my head to control the bleeding. That towel was all you could find in the heat of the moment. Your driving made it clear you were on a mission. Arriving at the office, we were whisked to an examining room where Dr. Magee worked his magic on my face. With my eyes covered, I continually pulled your arm and body closer to my face for comfort. You countered with, "The doctor can't do his work if I am any closer."

Ten stitches later and with a clean white dressing, we drove home. I was exhausted. I didn't eat dinner, and put myself to bed at 7 p.m. That day was over!

Thanks to your quick thinking, and suppressed reaction of shear panic, we both survived that home accident. I love you for being there and handling the situation as calmly as your feelings allowed on an otherwise uneventful weekday afternoon.

Thank you so much for being my Mommy.

Joanie

1958

Dear Mom,

This letter is devoted solely to your beloved mother, Florence Truby Gable, and my cherished grandmother. It seemed like I lost my Grandma Gable much too early in life. She was only fifty-eight years old. Certainly, you felt the same way about the loss. You were not even in your mid thirties this year.

I remembered many things about Grandma Gable. Every Sunday, we gathered around the large ornate dining room table at the Gable's home on Crescent Drive in Altoona near Baker Mansion for the midday meal. The menu always featured Southern fried chicken with all the side dishes. Grandma was an excellent cook and prepared the world's most delicious golden brown fried chicken which was crunchy on the outside, and soft, tender, and juicy on the inside. My favorite part of the chicken was the leg with its moist dark meat. The mashed potatoes were smooth, creamy, and loaded with real butter, just the way I preferred them.

In the spring of this year, Grandma Gable presented me with a dazzling white ruffled dress, packaged neatly in a Gable's Department Store dress box. I felt like a little princess in my frilly frock, the most special garment I ever owned. The dress was meant for important occasions such as Sunday morning church services and school pictures.

During the month of July, we vacationed at the Jersey Shore as usual. As the weeks progressed, Grandma began to feel sick. With her loss of appetite and Dad's strong recommendation to see a doctor upon returning to Altoona, we still enjoyed our time at the beach as always.

By late September, Grandma was gone. Cancer had spread throughout her internal organs, and even surgery could not improve her condition. Sitting by her bedside in the hospital each and every afternoon for support, you watched your beloved mother slip away. Of course, you were too young at thirty-three to experience this kind of deep and profound loss. As a first grader, in the fall of the school year, I was oblivious to your needs and concerns. Apparently, you soldiered through each day as fall leaves gave way to snow flurries.

By Christmas of 1958, Grandpa Gable, your much-admired father, was remarried with a pretty young wife, who brought a young daughter to the marriage. Most likely, your grief and confusion weighed you down. However, you continued to shine at holiday time as the new hostess for Christmas dinner.

God bless you for allowing us to see you as happy, and not sad, these past few months.

I love you dearly.

Joanie

1959

Dear Mom,

Life at 3503 Fort Roberdeau Avenue is predictable each and every day. Daddy drives his Chevy to work at Parsons Agency and sells real estate while Gingy, Georgia and I attend school. You have created a life at home, alone, all day as you read, fold laundry, tidy up the house, and fix meals.

Gingy excelled as a student at Theodore Roosevelt Junior High School. Georgia was a popular and well-liked sixth grader at Baker School this year. Second grade moved along quite well for me with Mrs. Merkle as my teacher. For fun, Mrs. Merkle quizzed us, one by one, on the Brain Teasers from *Highlights Magazine*. The daily exercise warmed up our brains and prepared us for a day of thinking. I loved the challenge.

At home, we ate dinner promptly at 6 p.m. every evening. Daddy sat at the head of the table, with you and Gingy on the window side of the table, and Georgia and me on the kitchen counter side. The space for dining was small, but we all seemed to fit with a little squeezing. My favorite meal that you prepared was broiled lamb chops with a side of baked potatoes. Sometimes we were treated to a Betty Crocker yellow box-mix cake for dessert. My tummy did a happy dance when you served cake for dessert.

Homework was a must before television watching and bedtime. For entertainment, we enjoyed viewing shows that included *Walt Disney Presents*, *The Ed Sullivan Show*, and *I Love Lucy*. You and I adored television watching in our cozy playroom. The time passed by very fast, and the stories transported us to imaginary places. Comedies with stars such as Lucille Ball, made us laugh from our bellies.

My favorite toy was the Barbie doll, new this year. Barbie was a gift from Boonie at Christmas. Your sister, Boonie had access to all the best toys and games since she lived and worked in New York City. My Barbie doll had a long, silky, blond ponytail and a black sparkly evening dress with a mermaid silhouette. Barbie was beautiful from the tip of her shiny yellow hair to her dainty red-painted toe nails.

The most fun I had each week was playing outside with Waggie and the other neighborhood children. We enjoyed pick up games of kickball, hide and seek, and red rover. Each game began with an Eeny, Meeny, Miny Moe to pick team captains. A pick- up game of kickball was a metaphor for life. We had to select players for each team (staffing), referee our own games (negotiations), and play by the rules (honesty).

Church service every Sunday morning was a must in our family. We faithfully observed the weekly schedule and sat in the same pew at the First United Presbyterian Church of Altoona. As a squirmy kid, I had a tough time sitting still for a full hour. If Aunt Louise was there, she drew pictures of adorable babies or bunnies that amused me and helped pass the time during a long serious sermon delivered by the pastor at the pulpit.

You continue to make my life predictable and safe. I love you so much.

Joanie

Our house in Altoona

Mommy and Joanie
May 4, 1952

Mommy and Joanie
Summer 1952

Gingy, Joanie, Georgia
Christmas 1952

Grandpa Gable and Joanie
1953

Louise	Florence	Helen
Parsons	Parsons	Basler

July 1954

Joanie at age 2
Fall 1954

Joanie at the Jersey shore
1955

Living room desk

Florence Truby Gable
1958

1960's

Notes for the Reader

The decade of the 1960's produced noticeable changes in my personality as an emerging adolescent. My mother's personality also grew and matured with each new experience. Although she continued to handle herself with poise and elegance, she showed signs of cracking around the edges as evidenced by nervousness and stress. With my new-found boldness in saying and doing things that had a tendency to cross a line, we clashed. This outcome is typical in any mother-daughter relationship as the women involved learn to navigate the waters of compromise between protection and independence.

As you read the letters from the 1960's, be aware of the changing winds, both for my mother and for me. We still enjoyed our light-hearted moments of laughter and fun, but our actions and behaviors moving forward were becoming a product of all we were viewing on television and through films, as well as from music and literature. If nothing else, I was becoming much more aware of the larger world outside of Altoona, and it brought on a restlessness to grow up and to move on with my life.

Having said that, I was still an innocent teen enjoying time with girlfriends, my school life, the children's choir at church, and a couple of boyfriends along the way.

1960

Dear Mom,

I feel as though I have morphed into the kind of child only a mother could love. My hair is unruly, my teeth are overlapped and crowded in my mouth, and my eyesight is so bad, I need glasses all my waking hours. My shape has earned me the nickname "Chubbers" from Georgia.

In the academic arena, I knew you were coming home from parent-teacher conferences with reports that I was not achieving grades that reflected my potential. Mrs. Eisenburg, my hard-driving task master of a third-grade teacher, had placed me in the very back row in class. Each morning she drilled us on phonics rules, with examples, on the front chalkboard. I felt lost some days. I wondered if I was missing something the other students could see clearly. To everyone's surprise, after failing the school eye test, I did need glasses. What a difference in my world! Now, I could actually see the flag at the top of the neighborhood flagpole as well as the classroom chalkboard. Soon my grades began to improve.

Thank goodness for you and my loyal friend, Waggie. Waggie and I loved to run home from school each afternoon, change clothes quickly, and meet outside for a couple hours of rough play. Our favorite games included hard-hitting tackle football, kickball, and hide and seek. The time between school and dinner whizzed by in the blink of an eye.

The best meal you made, that I got only once a year for my birthday, was spaghetti and meat sauce along with a multi-colored cake for dessert. That meal made my mouth water and my taste buds tingle. The birthday meal was filling, warm, and comforting. The rest of the year, we followed Dad's strict eating rules for athletes: low in carbohydrates, plenty of red meat, only one starch, vegetables, salad, and a light dessert such as ice cream each night.

You are still my advocate and support. I know you love me and I love you. We always sit side by side in the last pew in church on Sunday mornings. We laugh out loud at silly television comedies, and we rate Ritz Crackers with American Cheese slices as the world's most delicious and satisfying snack.

You're my favorite Mommy.

Joanie

1961

Dear Mom,

It's the spring of third grade, and I'm about to go on my first date. Although Bobby and I are classmates in Mrs. Eisenberg's room at Baker School, we really never talk to each other.

So, it surprised me one day at school when Bobby asked me to go to the movies with him the following Saturday afternoon. I asked your permission and you happily agreed. In fact, the date was so important to you, I received a lovely new outfit, something that almost never happened as the third daughter in the family. Hand-me-downs were the rule in our home.

The new clothes really gave the day a special feel. You selected a look for me from Gable's Department Store, and I loved it. The slacks were made of a soft lavender polished cotton. The pants were paired with a coordinating white knit shirt and a lavender kitten applique on the left shoulder area. The latest in children's fashion was perfect for a springtime afternoon outing. Your simple act of kindness revealed to me the importance of always dressing appropriately for the occasion.

On the day of our "date," Bobby rode his bicycle to our house, about a half mile, parked it inside the garage for safe keeping, and we walked the three blocks to the Rivoli Theater. I don't remember any conversation that afternoon. However, when we arrived at the box office, Bobby proudly pulled out his wallet from a back pocket and showed me two crisp one dollar bills he carried to fund our date.

With two tickets in hand, purchased for fifty cents each, we enjoyed an afternoon double feature. Who knows what we actually watched. It could have been a Western, a comedy, or a romance. It really didn't matter. All the kids in my neighborhood hung out at the theater every Saturday afternoon. The weekly double features got us out of the house for several hours, and the time away from home gave the Mommies their much- needed break.

When the show ended, we walked the three blocks back to my house, again in silence. Once arriving at our house, Bobby mounted his bike and headed for home.

The perfect date, with the perfect outfit, on a perfect spring afternoon. Did Bobby and I speak again in school the following week? Not sure. As dates go, though, this one was hard to beat. Bobby set the bar very high--perfect gentleman, quiet companion, and loaded with cash.

Thanks for being the Mom who takes third grade dating seriously.

I love you so much.

Joanie

1962

Dear Mom,

You know best that I am an outdoor girl who enjoys endless hours of kickball and hide & seek with the neighborhood kids. I also enjoy solitary activities such as roller skating, twirling the hoola hoop around my waist and knees, and riding a bicycle.

This year, I turned ten. It was a milestone birthday, for sure. The most special birthday gift would be a new two-wheel bicycle to call my own. Up to this point, I have been borrowing Gingy's and Georgia's bikes, all of them used and littering our garage. Something brand new, just for me, would make all my dreams come true.

On the day of my tenth birthday, I discovered the most special gift of all--a shiny new bicycle in lavender waiting for me to ride. It was a Schwinn--the most coveted brand of the day. You listened to my one and only idea for a really special birthday gift this year.

Riding my new bike made me feel free and confident. I mastered trick riding--steering and turning without the use of handles, just shifting body weight. My route took me down Fort Roberdeau Avenue, to Aldrich Avenue, with a left on East Holmes Avenue, then to Shelly Avenue, and back toward home by way of Ward Avenue. I felt like a super hero whizzing past familiar neighborhood houses without using my hands to steer on that flashy new mode of transportation.

With the April breezes whipping through my hair, and the fresh scent of clean air on my face, nothing could stop me now. That feeling was pure freedom, and I emerged as the master of my universe whenever I mounted my new bike.

Best birthday ever, thanks to you.
I love you, Mommy.

Joanie

November 22, 1963

Dear Mom,

Sixth grade is a typical year for me. I still wear glasses and heavy corrective shoes every waking hour. The days all go by in much the same manner except one day in November.

Just as Miss Wilson's class at Baker School began the afternoon routine, there was a subtle knock at the large oak door. Miss Wilson approached, opened it, and stepped into the hallway for less than a minute. Our principal, Miss Moore, delivered a shocking blow. Miss Wilson returned to the room, stood erect before our class sporting a print shirtwaist dress and sturdy black shoes. Tears welled up in her eyes.

Miss Wilson conveyed a message of loss and grief. Our youthful and movie-star handsome president, John F. Kennedy, had been shot and killed by a sniper in Dallas, Texas, that afternoon. He was dead. Our class sat motionless and silent. We didn't know much, but anytime there was an unexpected death, the seriousness of the situation weighed heavily on young minds. No one dared to move or speak.

Miss Wilson did her best to explain what she knew while letting the news sink into our sixth-grade brains. We were numb. I needed to know more, but did not dare to ask even a nearby classmate about the real meaning of Miss Wilson's message. I could only assume that our parents would shoulder the responsibility of interpreting the deeper meaning of this event. Dad might be happy as his politics were deeply conservative, while you have always been more in tune with social issues and justice for all Americans--the Kennedy perspective.

Jackie Kennedy was your idol. Young, slim, and stylish, Mrs. Kennedy wore only designer clothing and presented herself like royalty. Also, she embodied every American woman's idea of poise and elegance. Mrs. Kennedy was only thirty-four years of age, and now widowed with two young children. By comparison, you are thirty- nine years of age, the mother of three active daughters, and very much an involved wife. Although your life experiences are worlds apart, you and Jackie Kennedy are contemporaries. What does this shift in leadership mean to you? Perhaps, the idealism of the Kennedy Administration is gone forever.

In spite of this tragedy, I am still your happy, carefree, little girl who loves her friends, outdoor play, and the familiarity of the neighborhood around Baker School.

I love you very much.

Joanie

Spring, 1964

Dear Mom,

I notice that you have a habit of drinking beer. You start in the early afternoon and continue until you are barely normal at our 6 p.m. dinner time.

Thoughts race through my sixth-grade brain. Should I say something to you? Do you know that I have watched your behavior for quite a while and believe you to be two different people? The mommy I know best is kind and thoughtful, as well as encouraging. The other mommy is wobbly, slurs her speech, and is unaware that I'm in the house. You are like two different people. Courage is building to say something to you.

The daily drinking must be the reason why you don't volunteer at my school like the other mothers. In fact, you decline all invitations to leave the house in the evening for activities, meetings, or gatherings unless you can drink with your friends. This behavior limits your after-hours involvements to only house parties in the neighborhood.

This afternoon, I approached you in the kitchen to ask you to stop drinking beer each day. I thought substituting orange juice or tea for your beloved Miller would be a smart alternative. Unfortunately, my plan backfired as you became angry, annoyed, and told me that *your* drinking was none of *my* business.

My whole being stood humiliated in that moment. It was all I could do to turn on my heel and walk straight to my bedroom, close the door quietly, and think about what I had just done to make you so angry. Although you didn't yell at me, your words cut me like a knife with bitterness, something I had never experienced from you in the past.

Would we ever move beyond this confrontation and be friends again? Truly, your reaction stunned me and the tone of your voice sent chills through me. In all my twelve years, you've never been so mean to me. Silently, in my room, I'm now trying to process the kitchen conversation and make sense of it.

I wonder what all this means. I have no idea why drinking is so bad and I'm scared that our relationship will change forever.

I am confused and sad in this moment.

Still, I love you deeply, Mom.

Joanie

April, 1965

Dear Mom,

Turning thirteen is every girl's dream. Finally, I arrived at teenage status. The birthday party you hosted for me this month was epic. You took the role of party planner very seriously and the results were outstanding. Our relationship was back on track, which made both of us feel comfortable and relaxed once again.

The evening was filled with girls *and* boys in our living room and dining room. Your role, pleasantly accepted, was to chaperone a group of my friends for two hours. The party was your way of helping me, the shy girl at school, mix and mingle with my peers. Way to go, Mom.

The party was unforgettable for two reasons. First, because we turned off all the lights to dance in the dark while you sat quietly in the kitchen reading a book with the door closed. The second feature of this party that blew my mind was that you had arranged for a white sheet cake with decorative horses all over the top as a surprise. Horses were my passion and you had indulged me with a few private riding lessons over the years.

This was what you missed in the living room this evening. The group of girls gathered in the dining room to whisper about the boys. Someone continuously played "Unchained Melody" by the Righteous Brothers on the record player in the living room all night. Slow, romantic music played throughout the entire party. With the start of each new turn on the same song, the boys walked to the dining room, asked the girls to dance, then held them and swayed for three minutes. When the music ended, we all returned to our separate corners just like prize fighters between rounds.

The only exception to this routine was Waggie and his girlfriend, Janet. They chose not to dance at all. Instead, they made out on the living room couch the entire evening. I danced appropriately with Mark. My best friend, Nancy, danced all evening with Joe. To my knowledge,

none of the dancers fooled around. I was decked out in a school outfit-
-blue corduroy jumper and white collared blouse. Tres chic! The other
girls wore anything from shorts to skirts, all representing mid 1960's
attire.

In the end, the lights came on, we enjoyed the cake, and everyone
departed for home.

Truly, this was my most memorable birthday. Junior High School,
turning thirteen, and dancing slowly with a boy have all contributed to
my new level of maturity. But still, I am sporting glasses, braces, and
corrective shoes like a grade-school kid.

Thanks for being that cool mom who let me have a cool party.

I love you.

Joanie

1966

Dear Mom,

A full year of Home Economics at Roosevelt Junior High School is exactly what I need. The course offerings include cooking, sewing, child care, and decorating. Each of these exploratory classes, one quarter each, have captivated my attention and imagination. Plus, I excel at cooking, sewing, child care, and decorating. Who knew those talents lay just beneath the surface of my quiet junior high personality.

In cooking class, we learned how to make tuna salad. I repeated the recipe for you at home, and you devoured it. Thanks, Mom, for being such a willing taste tester. We both agreed it tasted delicious.

Sewing class also intrigued me. I think the connection to math was the deciding factor. Math had always been my best subject in school. We made two matching pillow cases, and an A-line skirt. My garment was meant to be fashionable with a yellow background and an orange dotted Swiss pattern. Very mod, in my opinion. Too bad the skirt never really fit. It was tight in the hips and baggy in the waist. I had even purchased an orange ribbed knit poor boy shirt to wear with the new skirt. Looks like my really cool outfit would never see the light of day.

As for child care, I adored working with doll babies while changing diapers and pretending to bathe them. The curriculum consisted of providing a clean, safe, environment for our "babies." You can imagine the hours of fun we enjoyed in that school classroom "playing dolls" for forty minutes a day several days a week.

For Interior Design, we created scaled representations of our own bedrooms and little cut outs of our furniture. Then, we experimented with room arrangements. Since my bedroom was very tiny, I had no other lay outs to try. My only pieces of furniture were a single bed, a small desk, and a child-size dresser. With two windows and two closet doors, I was stumped as to how to put my three pieces of furniture in any other formation besides the way it was now.

You could see that I had talent in sewing, and because of my new-found passion you purchased a used sewing machine for me to motivate me to do more clothing construction. I was thrilled to have my very own sewing machine. The next step would be sewing lessons at the Singer Sewing Center in the Pleasant Valley Shopping Center.

I love you so much for encouraging my new hobby.

Joanie

Fall, 1967

Dear Mom,

This is the year I enter Altoona High School for students in grades ten to twelve. I am extremely nervous. The stories on the street describe how the senior boys check out the incoming sophomore girls as they approach the main entrance to the building on the first day of school. Fortunately, that never happened. Must have been an urban legend.

You and I still loved the same things in life such as popular music, nightly television shows, and movies. Under the heading of popular music, I had been listening to The Doors and "Light My Fire" over and over again in my quiet and private room over the garage, Gingy's old bedroom. The Beatles had done something groundbreaking too, with "Sgt. Pepper's Lonely Hearts Club Band." The Rolling Stones, also known as the bad boys of the rock and roll world, recorded songs this year including "Ruby Tuesday" and "Let's Spend the Night Together." Although the lyrics shocked many people, you didn't seem to mind and allowed me to play those songs many times each evening in my room with the door closed.

Our taste in television programming included *The Fugitive* with David Janssen. He portrayed a true leading man with good looks and the intelligence to get out of any situation. The show provided riveting drama that you and I enjoyed each week. Our favorite movies during the year included *The Graduate* with Dustin Hoffman, *Bonnie and Clyde* with Warren Beatty, and *Cool Hand Luke* starring Paul Newman. Hollywood's leading men perfectly fulfilled the description of handsome hunks.

The most troubling part of our world this year was that the United States had sent 475,000 soldiers to Vietnam to fight for democracy. North Vietnam had invaded the south where people lived freely. Now, a war had broken out and we were helping the South fight the North. The year 1967 developed into a very confusing time for our country, being at war on foreign soil and not being able to detect enemies from friends among the Vietnamese people. I heard stories from classmates at school who had siblings, relatives, and neighbors stationed in Vietnam. Those soldiers came home changed in many ways. They now drank alcohol and smoked marijuana, and they seemed zoned out and unproductive every day.

Fortunately, we are very close in our special *simpatico* way. With Gingy and Georgia out of the house, and my new digs in the room over the garage, life is good. We take long walks on weekends, through the neighborhood and beyond, just to get some exercise and have a conversation. Saturday lunch usually includes Sheetz' hoagies that you pick up on your way home from the hair salon. I could not ask for a better relationship with you, Mom.

I love you so much.

Joanie

1968

Dear Mom,

March of 1968 is a hopeful time for our family with Gingy is on track to marry Steve in our hometown. Wedding plans had been finalized for a Saturday afternoon in late March at the First United Presbyterian Church. Georgia and I would serve as the only bridesmaids. My dress and shoes are a dream come true--a real vision in pink.

The stunningly beautiful silk dress I wore that day made me feel grown up and important; it felt like something Jackie Kennedy would have selected from her own wardrobe on that cool grey day in March. It was an honor and a privilege to stand up for Gingy on her wedding day.

At almost sixteen years old, I knew a whole lot more than you might have guessed. For example, I understood that Gingy selected the church basement for the wedding reception, a venue that strictly prohibited the serving and consumption of alcohol. Gingy made this decision to avoid any temptation on your part to drink to excess and draw unwanted attention *your* way on *her* big day.

On the day of the wedding, our pastor officiated a short and sweet ceremony. Gingy looked lovely, in a conservative teacher kind of way, while wearing a simple white satin street-length dress and short veil. During the final blessing, Gingy and Steve knelt and received a message of love and hope which filled my heart.

The day was flawless. Georgia and I performed on cue as attendants in our pink silk coat dresses and matching heels. On that special day, and wearing those clothes, I was coming more and more to my own realization that we were all growing older in our own ways. You, with a few added pounds and thinning hair, and me with a strong desire to experience the world beyond Altoona.

For now, though, I was still the fly on the wall that heard and saw everything. The wedding weekend was emotional with tears, accusations, and unspoken words. Maybe you suppressed feelings of disappointment for Gingy and think she settled for a man she didn't know well enough or didn't seem to love deeply. Perhaps, the marriage would not last a lifetime. Nothing is ever guaranteed. Maybe, you wanted something more for your first born daughter. I can't read your mind.

All I know for sure is that the entire day you displayed your usual grace and poise, and for that we are all very grateful.

I love you.

Joanie

1969

Dear Mom,

Something happens to teenagers in their senior year of high school that transforms them from kind rule-following children to experimental and rebellious semi-adults. My break from conformity happened in the fall of this year as a seventeen-year-old girl, a scenario you had witnessed twice before with Gingy and Georgia.

In the fall of our senior year of high school, my best friend, Nancy, was selected to take college-level courses at the Altoona branch campus of Penn State University. This privilege came with a bona fide college I.D. With a newly-acquired form of identification came entrance to all the college dances and access to college men. An evening of music, dancing, and mingling materialized as our weekend plan.

That Friday night, Nancy and I dressed up in our best school outfits to experience a coveted weekly event at the Altoona Campus. It was a large dark space with loud music and plenty of guys to ask us to dance. We enjoyed our share of dances, both fast and slow. It was the perfect evening of entertainment.

As we left the venue to drive home in your car, I accidentally backed into a low post in the parking lot. Darn it! Now what? "Just keep driving" was my first thought, and confirmed by Nancy. I swear neither Nancy nor I drank a drop of any beverages that evening. We were dancers, not drinkers.

Nancy and I concocted a story that we would both stick to religiously, if asked. We planned to pretend we didn't know a thing about the dented bumper. As friends, keeping our pact, we would just let you assume you did the damage to your own car.

A few days later, you asked me about the damage to the bumper. I played dumb. You left the topic alone. Days later, you approached me again with the bumper question. Apparently, you drove to the Altoona Campus and found the post I hit in the parking lot with white paint as evidence. To that face-to-face accusation, I confessed to the damage. Then, in your ultimate mother wisdom, you confessed something of your own. You replied, "I never did drive to the campus." In that moment, you busted me. I had been caught in a lie I created myself. Not much of an actress, I guess.

The entire situation was my fault from start to finish. You outsmarted me, although it didn't take much. I certainly conceded to your mothering skills; you know a thing or two about dealing with teenage daughters. Well played, Mom.

With love and respect to you. . .

Joanie

Joanie in third grade
1960-61

Joanie in fourth grade
1961-62

Easter
1969

Joanie as a high school senior
1969-70

1970's

Notes for the Reader

During the 1970's, a shift happened in how my mother and I interacted. As I became a young adult, having graduated from high school in June of 1970, she let go a bit. I started my adult life in Ohio as an undergraduate student at Kent State University. I married Vito in 1973, became a classroom teacher, attended graduate school, and gave birth to Kristina in 1978. By contrast, my mother was an empty nester, and she spent more and more time in her vacation condominium in Florida and less time in Pennsylvania in my childhood home.

Mom and I stayed in touch with letters, greeting cards, occasional phone conversations, and a few visits to Altoona. Those trips to Altoona were few and far between, just meant to touch base with family, recharge my batteries and celebrate holidays. Also, they served as a much-needed break from the rigors of higher education and my special needs students in the classroom. Mom understood the draw to come home to family, and she always made Vito and me feel extremely welcome, comfortable, and appreciated.

By the close of 1979, I was completely exhausted by work, mothering, and the final draft of my doctoral dissertation. It all took its toll. I realize now that I was no comfort or support to my dear mother in her time of need. She, too, had her own worries, concerns, and heartache. Sincerely, I wish I had understood then what I know to be true now.

May, 1970

Dear Mom,

You have an odd way of scaring me at night. When I came home at midnight, we had a confrontation like no other. I had spent the past several hours at a birthday party for Ed's friend and sipped beer all evening. As you know, Ed and I have dated most of my senior year of high school. Yes, I was tipsy.

Promptly at 11:55 p.m., Ed pulled into our driveway to drop me off. To my surprise the entire house was lit up like a Christmas tree. That never happened. Usually, I tiptoed into the house and up the stairs in the dark, so as not to arouse you and Dad. I am a Zen Master in the art of quiet entries while slipping into my room undetected. My entire senior year of high school, each Friday and Saturday night, while out on dates with Ed or babysitting a neighborhood family with three boys, my entrance was flawless. And now, the two of you had stayed up well past your bedtime to watch television in the playroom.

Suddenly, I wondered how to solve this problem. Should I circle the block for thirty minutes with Ed and sneak in quietly after you and Dad have gone to bed? Or, should I make my midnight curfew and enter the room a little wobbly? There would be a price to pay either way.

I decided to try to walk past you as steadily as possible and say "good night" as I swayed to the stairway. Darn it! You detected my unsteady gait instantly. You have the super power of spotting an inebriated person a mile away. Of course, the scene was uncomfortable. The overhead spotlights in the ceiling focused on me like I was a criminal being questioned for murder.

Another telltale sign of my impaired state was the unbuttoned fly of my Levi's button front jeans. Apparently, when I used the bathroom at the party, my fingers were in no condition to re-attach all six buttons of the fly. Fortunately, the long baggy tee shirt I wore covered the error. However, my appearance was uncharacteristically sloppy.

I made my way past the two of you without speaking, while you spewed unrecognizable language at me. I think you shouted something like this: "What happened to you?" Dad didn't say much. His focus was on a televised basketball game. Playoffs, perhaps?

After closing my bedroom door for the night, and finally feeling safe, you swung it wide open again to yell at me even more. I never did catch everything you said, only that you grabbed my left wrist, twisted my arm to the side, and actually checked for track marks. Really, Mom? Drugs? Not this girl. I am a needle phobic human being, and have been since I was a toddler. Try again in the morning with your loud tongue-lashing accusations after you've sobered up a bit.

The following morning made me tense and anxious. I had to wait until after noon to sit and endure the "talk" from both you and Dad since Dad's office hours included Saturday mornings. It was short and painless, thank goodness. I think you both realized it was an isolated incident and you didn't need to drill me on Pennsylvania law when it came to eighteen-year old high school students drinking beer. The legal drinking age was clearly twenty-one. Lesson learned.

Obviously, I broke the rules last night, but you jumped to completely irrational conclusions. We both chipped away at the relationship we so cherish. Maybe that's what happens in the final year a teenager spends at home before college.

All I know is that you are my mother, flaws and all. I am your rule-breaking teen who made a bad choice at a party last night. Can we move past our embarrassing behavior and recapture our strong, loving, more-like-girlfriends bond? Truly, I hope so.

I love you so much.

Joanie

September, 1970

Dear Mom,

Today, I left home for college. My departure did not warrant any celebrations, long sorrowful good byes, not even any words of advice from you. Just Georgia and me heading west to Kent, Ohio, with Georgia behind the wheel of her navy blue Volkswagen. The car was loaded, mostly with my stuff for the dorm room. Georgia was returning to her furnished apartment in Kent and roommates Patty and Janine.

By four o'clock, we arrived at Koonce Hall in the Tri-Towers complex. My room, located on the second floor next to the always opening and closing elevator doors, would be shared with a girl named Debbie from New York City. Based on the the looks of the pristine space, I had arrived first.

Georgia and I unloaded the car and left my pile of belongings on the curb. She was in a hurry to see her friends, so I made four trips to the room to transport my clothing and other room necessities all alone. Help would have been appreciated, but I didn't ask.

After a couple of hours of unpacking and organizing, I had everything just as I wanted it in my half of the room. My bed for the next nine months, the lower half of a bunk, was smoothed over with a pale yellow chenille bedspread that made the room sunny. Clothes were arranged on hangers in the closet, drawers filled neatly with folded clothes, and desk supplies tucked away in the drawers of my new work space. On the desk, I displayed two small photos of my boyfriend Ed in twin gold frames, hinged in the middle. This served as a reminder of the life I left behind in Altoona where Ed lived and worked.

When I finished with my room, I dashed off to grab dinner in the cafeteria. To my surprise and disappointment, the dining hall was locked tightly for the night. Apparently, it had closed within the past thirty minutes. With no prospect of food for the next twelve hours, I walked back to my dorm room to wait, and finally fall asleep.

Breakfast was served promptly at 7 a.m. and I was one of the first in line at the cafeteria. While standing in place, I met two friendly and helpful girls, Bev and Donna, both from small communities in Ohio. We sat together over breakfast, shared information, and agreed to hang out the rest of the day.

All in all, my second day on campus turned out *much* better than the first. I miss you, and all that is familiar to me at home and in our neighborhood.

Hopefully, you will make the three and a half-hour drive to Kent and visit me very soon.

I love you.

Joanie

1971

Dear Mom,

Did you know that my roommate this past year at Kent State University was a drug dealer, and ran a successful business out of our shared dorm room in Koontz Hall the past nine months? Well, neither did I.

You never met Debbie, the young woman who shared this tiny space with me. From New York City, Debbie was worldly and a transfer student. She was anything but a fresh-faced eighteen year old like me. As you well know from your time in New York City as a young woman, there is absolutely no comparison between the Big Apple and my quiet, uneventful hometown. Debbie and I were raised in completely different environments, and so we didn't hang out much together.

I discovered the drugs early one morning in May as I strode past our bank of built-in drawers that doubled as the dressers in our tiny room. Debbie's top drawer, typically the underwear drawer, was open. My brief glance revealed a space packed with numerous baggies, all filled with pills and marijuana.

That one brief discovery became my lightbulb moment. The profits from drug sales explained why Debbie always had pocket money when the rest of us budgeted every nickel of our meager allowances from home or part-time paychecks. Drugs were the reason why strangers would knock on our room door every evening, enter, close the door, stay for only ten seconds, then leave. I observed this behavior for a full nine months from the study lounge opposite our room.

Clearly, the drugs factored into Debbie's repeated attempts to persuade me to try marijuana. You will be happy to hear, I was always reluctant to take Debbie up on her offer. Her words sounded like this: "When you are ready to try marijuana, I want to be the one to turn you on." That questionable invitation creeped me out in a major way.

Debbie was sophisticated, assertive, out spoken, and a successful small business owner--all the qualities I lacked. Clearly, I could have used your first impressions of Debbie back in September of last fall when I was putting down roots on my new university campus. Debbie was nice enough, but we just never connected as friends. Was it me, or was it Debbie? You would have provided the correct perception from the start.

Thank goodness, your baby girl is still your baby girl. Next year, as a sophomore, I will be living in single housing, and I already have a room reserved for me in Leebrick Hall. No more roommates for me!

I love you and miss you.

Joanie

September, 1972

Dear Mom,

By now, I'm in my final year at Kent State University, having condensed four years of coursework for a Bachelor's Degree in Education into three by enrolling for classes each summer. I love the fast-paced world of academia and don't want to take the traditional three-month breaks each summer. I'm on a roll, and on track to graduate in August of next year. As long as Dad continues to pay the tuition bills, I'm happy with this arrangement.

My steady boyfriend has been Vytenis "Vito" Kuraitis for the past two years, thanks to an introduction from a mutual friend, Bev, in the fall of 1970. Ed and I broke up in November of that year with a face-to-face conversation in the playroom over Thanksgiving weekend. I met Vito in early November of 1970 and wanted to pursue a relationship with him. You adore Vito, having graciously hosted his visits to Altoona on several occasions in the past year. It's no surprise that you fell in love with him, too, given his natural charm, intelligence, and quick wit.

In the past, Vito and I had discussed our life as a married couple. We seemed very compatible with one another and shared the same values for family, home, work, and success. Now, seeing Vito after a break of nearly a month, brought up the topic of marriage once again.

While relaxing in my dorm lounge, on a dingy upholstered sofa, Vito said to me: "Do you still want to get married?" My reply was, "I do. Do you?" To that answer, Vito said, "I guess." Although I didn't feel his sincerity or warmth in that moment, Vito jumped up and proclaimed that we must drive to J.B. Robinson Jewelers in Cleveland to look at rings.

Later that afternoon, I selected a simple ring set in gold with a half carat diamond in the center and four tiny diamonds around the main stone, There were touches of black around the diamonds to highlight their sparkle, and an engagement guard which would be used as the wedding ring at the ceremony. The two rings would eventually be soldered together into one ring. I selected a complementary gold ring with touches of black for Vito, and had it engraved inside with the Lithuanian words for "I love you." Vito and his family continued to speak Lithuanian at home as their first language, so the inscription was especially sentimental to me and, hopefully, to Vito.

I look forward to my next visit to Altoona when I can show you the ring and get your reaction to it. For now, know that I love the ring, and look forward to the wedding in September of next year. I know how much you adore Vito so this news should make you very happy.

Thank you for sharing my joy.

Joanie

December 25, 1972

Dear Mom,

Today is Christmas. Oh, how I love this day. It's my favorite in the entire year.

Our most blessed twenty-four hours of the entire year began with a candle light service at the First United Presbyterian Church in Altoona last evening. After a good night's sleep, we all enjoyed the beautifully-wrapped gifts, arranged in colorful piles under the tree. The scent of roasting turkey in the house all day enveloped me with warmth and comfort. Later, we happily scarfed up your fabulous dinner with all the side dishes served promptly at 6 p.m.

Your dinner included a plump turkey with stuffing, mashed potatoes, dried corn from a can (but still delicious), and cranberry sauce that you made from scratch. Your sugar cookies were the best part of the meal. Another treat was that Grandma Parsons shared dinner with us on holidays, so this year was no exception. As usual, Grandma gave our family a decorative tin of her homemade cookies including my favorite, orange cookies with the soft texture and the fresh, sweet orange glaze, and aroma. They melted on my tongue in the most delicious combination of sweet and citrus-tart flavors.

Today was the day you presented Gingy, Georgia and me with the most stunning gold bracelets with semi-precious stones. My new piece of jewelry became the perfect compliment to my gold engagement ring from Vito and happily worn on the left hand the past three months. Because of the ring, I have been keeping my nails polished at all times in various shades of pink. Today was my last Christmas celebration as a single young woman of twenty. Next year at this time I expect to be married and honoring this religious celebration as Mrs. Vito Kuraitis.

Christmas always winds down after dinner when Georgia leaves for the evening to meet friends. The rest of us sit comfortably in the living

room and chat, bathed in the relaxation of our turkey comas.
I love making memories with you, Mom.

Joanie

September, 1973

Dear Mom,

Since I have been home on break, between college graduation and my wedding in a couple of weeks, we have been enjoying long walks together most days. This afternoon was especially entertaining as we did the usual walk around our Mansion Park neighborhood.

As we walked, you became quiet. I noticed that your hands were tense, almost to the point of mangling one another. Then, after a silent spell, you timidly offered these words, "maybe we should have a talk." Clearly, we were in the homestretch with my wedding only days away. Was this the sex talk? If so, shouldn't you have broached that topic when I was twelve with some nebulas story about birds and bees? Or, was this the talk about how to be a good wife, circa 1950, and the rules you and your friends followed? In that case, I wasn't interested in sleeping in "His" and "Hers" twin beds, putting dinner on the table promptly at 6 p.m. every evening, and stroking my husband's ego every chance I got without appearing obvious. In either case, I was not ready to hear those stories that perfect fall afternoon.

So, without ever skipping a beat, I replied, "What do you want to know?" With those words, you laughed, I laughed, and we both realized that the talk was not going to happen. I'm not a worldly person, but marital advice from you would have altered our relationship. My eyes were already searing at the images you might have created in my mind. Let's pretend this conversation never happened.

Quickly, we shifted back to chatter about friends, movies, books, and music--our usual topics. Our *simpatico* rhythm had returned to normal. Wedding plans were done, thanks to you. You made it so easy for me to be a bride. Every detail and bill was attended to by you. All I was ever expected to do was meet a photographer in July for the newspaper photo and eventually write my own thank you notes after the event. No fuss, no worries, no drama. I never questioned your decisions because of our similar tastes. So, I'm thankful this wedding will be a breeze.

Looking forward to the big day very soon. I hope you are as happy as you seem this pleasant afternoon.

I love you so very much, Mom.

Joanie

1975

Dear Mom,

You and I are both huge fans of the writer Erma Bombeck and her humor. Some of our favorite quotes from Erma's newspaper columns and books include the following: "dryers eat socks" and "housework, if done properly, can kill you." Those lines make us smile and chuckle in a knowing way each and every time we recite them to one another face-to-face. Clearly, Erma's prose represents housework humor at its best.

I'm still enjoying my first full-time permanent teaching assignment at Richardson Elementary School in Cuyahoga Falls, Ohio. There are ten boys assigned to my classroom, ranging in grade from second to sixth. Each boy has been diagnosed with either a learning or a behavior disability. My classroom functions like a tight ship, with ten students and nine reading groups. That style of management, learned by observation, must be a carryover from Dad's days in the Navy and how he expected our home to function while I was a child.

Vito was appointed Personnel Director at Centran Bank of Akron, earning a yearly salary of $13,000. Combined with my teaching salary of $8200, we live very well in our one-bedroom apartment on North Howard Avenue in Akron. The second-hand furniture you purchased at a moving sale, and trucked to our new home at your expense, fits perfectly.

Our friends include Harvey and Mary Lou Hanes, Lee Schurr, and Barry and Carol Brockenbraugh. Barry and Carol's little guy, Barry Junior, a three-year-old, always refers to us as Bito and Boanie. In his world, all names begin with the letter B.

Since I have been studying for my Master's degree in Guidance and Counseling, Vito and I spend every Sunday at the library on the campus of the University of Akron. I prepare most of my homework and class assignments on Sunday, to be ready for my evening classes during the week. Each school day, Monday through Friday, begins at 7:30 for me, and ends at 5:30 when Vito picks me up in front of my school building. In those ten hours, I complete all my lessons and preparations for the students each day. The hours make for a long and busy week, but as a newlywed couple, we don't mind a bit.

We have a very happy life here in Ohio. Wish we could see you more often, but I know the solo drive from Pennsylvania to Ohio makes you nervous and uncomfortable. So, we will wait and see you when Dad is able to drive both of you together.

I love you so much.

Joanie

April, 1976

Dear Mom,

On my birthday this year, you and Dad sent separate birthday cards. For me, this new division of attention is symbolizing your new life separated from Dad. After my wedding in 1973, I know life changed dramatically for you.

I understand why you gradually began spending longer stretches of time in Florida at the condominium, while Dad continued his life at the office in Altoona and with his passion for competitive tennis. Word spread that Dad and his secretary were involved in a romantic relationship. Call it what it really was--cheating or an affair. I know this news, which you learned just one month before my wedding day, broke your heart.

Later, you revealed to me that you wanted to commit suicide. I can't blame you for feeling so depressed. The pain must have been extremely intense. But, as you always did, you picked yourself up and carried on in the British fashion which was to put on a brave face and I admire that about you. I'm proud of you for creating a life for yourself in Florida with new friends, social tennis dates, lunch outings, and a new love interest of your own.

Now, however, at the age of twenty-four and on my birthday, my pain feels real. I cried silent tears realizing that you and Dad were not "Mom and Dad" anymore, but two separate entities in my life. You will continue to make your own decisions and not collaborate or discuss family matters with Dad. You are not a couple anymore. Understanding the redefined terms of the situation is my wake-up call to carry on and make sure I have a relationship with both of you in the future.

This issue has created sides in our family, but I'm in your corner. Gingy and Georgia seem cozy with Dad's girlfriend and okay with his decision. My perspective is very different. No man should treat his wife the way Dad treated you. Clearly, your heart has been broken, but you

are trying to move forward by creating a new life for yourself in Florida.
I am so sorry for you, Mom.

    Call me whenever you feel like talking.

    I love you very much.

Joanie

August 28, 1978

Dear Mom,

Our precious baby girl, Kristina, arrived today. She is perfect! Here's what you missed.

The labor pains (or discomfort) began at about 4 a.m. with some feelings in my lower back. It was not so bad, although I couldn't drift back to sleep. So, I showered, shampooed my hair, and shaved my legs. I waited until 7 a.m. to wake Vito and tell him that I thought the baby was coming. We timed contractions for the next two hours and called the doctor's office at 9:00 when it opened. Based on the regularity of the contractions, the doctor advised going straight to the hospital.

We arrived at Akron General Medical Center before 10:00 and waited for more signs from the baby we hoped would appear today, on her due date. But then the contractions seemed to slow, or even stop, altogether. We waited a very long, very boring few hours. My hunger pains accompanied by a growling stomach, were becoming obvious by noon. My only relief was sucking on ice chips. Vito left for a short time to enjoy a hearty meal at McDonald's while I continued to wait for more signals from the baby.

Finally, at about 4:30 p.m., things began to happen as I felt the need to push. Wow, this new phase of delivery pleased me after enduring hours of sweaty contractions. Although I studied Lamaze childbirth--and planned to have a natural birth--in the end I opted for the epidural (spinal) for numbing. Kristina appeared at about 5:20 p.m. and Dr. Morgan placed her on my stomach. I had the giggles and my very flabby belly created a few waves for Kristina.

Our beautiful baby girl had arrived. Every book on pregnancy referred to each and every birth as a miracle, with a fully-formed human being growing from a single cell. Kristina was our miracle with a fringe of dark fuzzy baby hair around her skull in back, creamy white skin, and bright blue eyes.

I know Vito used the wall phone in the hospital waiting area to contact you and Dad. We will eagerly await your visit with us and our new baby Kristina at our apartment in Kent in the next week or so. Can't tell you how excited I am for you to meet our beautiful new baby girl with her porcelain complexion.

Love you so much.

Joanie

Ed and Joanie on prom night
June 1970

Donna, Bev, and Joanie at Kent State University
1971

Joanie and Vito, the engaged couple
1972

Joanie and her new gold bracelet
Christmas 1972

Mom and Joanie
Spring 1973

Mom, Gingy, and Joanie at Baker Mansion
July 1973

Mr. and Mrs. William K. Parsons
request the honour of your presence
at the marriage of their daughter
Joan Kantner
to
Mr. Vytenis Petras Kuraitis
on Saturday, the fifteenth of September
nineteen hundred and seventy-three
at half after two o'clock
First United Presbyterian Church
Altoona, Pennsylvania

Reception
immediately following the ceremony
Blairmont Country Club
Hollidaysburg, Pennsylvania

73

Vito and Joanie on their wedding day
September 15, 1973

Mom and Joanie - Vito and Joanie's first apartment
in Akron, Ohio
Fall 1973

Mom and Joanie - Vito and Joanie's second apartment
in Uniontown, Ohio
Summer 1975

Mom with Baby Kristina
1978

New parents, Vito and Joanie
Spring 1979

1980's

Notes for the Reader

The 1980's presented both my mother and me with even more change and growth. During these years, my intimate family expanded to four, and we lived in Ohio, Texas, and Illinois. Our frequent moves came about because of Vito's career advancements.

For my mother, the changes included leaving Pennsylvania on a permanent basis and making Florida her home. After a few years in Florida, my mother joined us in Texas where Gingy and I were living. This way she could also be near all four of her beloved grandchildren. As the decade progressed, Vito's job took us to Illinois and its subsequent harsh winters. My mother chose to return to the sunshine of Florida once again.

Mom was now in her sixties and part of that revered group of citizens we call seniors. There were subtle and obvious declines in her health and appearance that I should have observed, and acted on, earlier. A few examples included her backwards sleeping schedule, unusual eating habits of only a couple minimal snacks per day, and a noticeable lack of interest in her usual favorite leisure activities such as reading. I wish I had been more persistent and persuasive in my approach with her and her needs because it pained me to witness how she neglected her health and well being.

January 19, 1982

Dear Mom,

My second baby girl arrived! Anne Parsons Kuraitis made her debut this morning at Akron General Medical Center. Weighing in at eight and a half pounds and measuring twenty-two inches in length she was considered a big baby. At each and every prenatal visit leading to Anne's birth the doctor confirmed I was carrying a boy based on the slow and strong heartbeat. Our newly-arrived bundle of joy fooled the doctor, for sure.

Again, just as with Kristina, the labor pains began in the middle of the night. We quickly dressed and delivered Kristina to our next door neighbor, Kay, a nurse and mother of four, and drove to the hospital at about 2:30 in the morning. Bank time and temperature signs along the route registered temperatures in the subzero ranges. Underground steam billowed in the still darkness as we made the sixty-mile journey to Akron for a delivery by my favorite group of OB-GYN doctors. By 7:30 a.m., Anne rested quietly in my arms. Our new baby girl was perfect in every way from her full head of dark hair to her deep blue eyes. Gratitude filled my heart for our new young doctor, Dr. Peterson, and his textbook delivery.

I desperately wanted to share this joyful experience with you today.

I hope you are loving Florida. I know you need to establish residency in that state in order to pursue a divorce, but I wish it didn't take so long. I'm not sure when you will visit your new baby granddaughter. Know that we welcome your presence any time you feel you can make the trip. Annie is a living doll. You will fall in love at first sight.

Please come see us very soon.

I love you and miss you.

Joanie

April 10, 1984

On this date in 1984, my mother wrote her own version of a love letter on the greeting card she sent to me for my thirty-second birthday.

Dearest Joanie,

Have the best birthday ever. How well I remember the day you were born. You were the best baby and now you are my best friend.
Life has a way of giving you back the good things.
Please know I love you and your precious family with all my heart.

Mom

September, 1985

Dear Mom,

Vito, Kristina, Anne and I are all happily settled in the Houston area, a real departure from our life a year ago in Cleveland, Ohio.

I'm thrilled you decided to sell your condominium in Gulfport, Florida, and move into our guest bedroom here in Kingwood, Texas. I still think you made the best decision to move closer to where Gingy and I live, and I love knowing that my daughters and Gingy's boys will be able to get to know you even better. Having a grandma nearby is the best living arrangement I could ever imagine. For me, knowing that you--my best friend--are so close makes everything perfect again.

I hoped you would have stayed longer than three months in our guest bedroom with the private bath, but I completely understand why you wanted to settle into your own quiet one-bedroom apartment. I know the noise of family life with two young children is too difficult for you at this stage in your life. Believe me, the noise sometimes bothers me, too.

For now, Annie and I adore stopping by your apartment for a popsicle and cards most afternoons. Go Fish is a family favorite of ours, thanks to the many years you and I played cards at the grey Formica kitchen table in Altoona. I know you're a fan of the homemade broccoli cheddar soup I sometimes bring with me made just for you.

So, we need to talk about this in person when I next see you. I'm a little worried. You don't look well. Your weight, which has always been a robust one hundred forty to one hundred fifty pounds, looks more like a gaunt one hundred and twenty pounds. Your face is drawn and you seem to be suffering hair loss.

Also, I've found out about the white wine that you purchase regularly by the jug at the local grocery store. My neighbor tipped me off to your almost daily routine since she shops multiple times per week feeding her family of five.

I'm not sure if your declining health is a loss of interest in living your life or some level of depression. I am virtually clueless regarding medical ailments and would like an instruction manual to understand you better. I think of life the way it was ten years ago, and I miss the vibrancy of your personality, your zest for living, and your interest in books, movies, and pop culture.

I love you so much.

Joanie

May 11, 1986

Dear Mom,

Today we celebrated Mother's Day with you. How pleased you seemed to be at the center of our love all day. Vito hosted Sunday brunch at the Houston Club which included Gingy and her family, our little family of four, and Georgia who flew in from Florida just to mark this occasion. In total, ten of us dined on well-prepared meals in a lavish setting of flowers, mood lighting, and elegant decor. The club even provided lilies for all the ladies. Lovely touch.

You looked especially beautiful in a white skirt suit and hot pink bow blouse. Your hair was styled to perfection, full and filled in on top with plenty of hair spray, our grooming product of choice. You were radiant today. Your smile lit up the room.

Among your four grandchildren--Billy (15), Jimmy (11), Krissie (7), and Annie (4)--you seem to enjoy Annie the most. She can be a clown with her crazy faces and voices, which always make you smile. Truly, this day was a celebration for all of us.

I hope you like the new red leather wallet, my special gift to you as a token of my love and devotion. Please forgive me for not telling you enough how much I love you and the blessing it is for me to have you as my mother.

We gifted Gingy with a homemade blueberry pie, her favorite food in all the world. This day was a celebration for Gingy, as well, to mark her birthday which happens tomorrow. She seemed overjoyed.

Family gatherings like this one are rare and treasured. We love dressing up, feasting on luscious meals, and relaxing into our food comas with the ever-present stories and loud laughter later in the day.

All is well on this Mother's Day, 1986.

Love you so very much.

Joanie

December 19, 1986

Dear Mom,

I'm so sad to be leaving you here in Texas. As you know, Vito has accepted and already begun working a new consulting position in Human Resources in Chicago. We leave later today, after Kristina finishes her third-grade day at Deerwood Elementary School. The two-week Christmas school break begins at three o'clock and that allows us time to transition to our new home in Chicago before she starts at her new school in early January.

As Annie and I visited with you one final time this December afternoon, we presented our family Christmas gift. It was a short, forest green, wool jacket to wear in the cooler months of winter, even in the south. The jacket, with its large round buttons, reminded me of the throw back styles of the 1940's, clothing you always admired. I'm glad you liked the gift our family gave you for Christmas. You seemed to enjoy opening the box and smiled and thanked us profusely. It has always been part of your DNA to be gracious.

By now, our furniture is loaded on the moving van, and the car will be towed to our new house in Naperville, Illinois. Vito and I offered you the opportunity to live with us in the new house which provides an in-law suite in the lower level. Your response was simple, but to the point. "Joanie, I can't live in the north again. My blood is thin, and it is just too cold." With that, we accepted your plans to move back to Florida next month.

Our family is writing a new chapter in our story as we journey to the Chicago area. Vito, Annie and I will pick up Kristina at school and drive to the airport to board a plane for O'Hare. Once there, Vito's thoughtful older brother, Al, will pick us up and we will stay at Pops' house in the city until our furniture arrives at Wood Court in Naperville on December 24th.

This is a time of change, anticipation, and hope. Clearly, we are

83

changing addresses, as are you. I anticipate a visit with you in Florida in the coming months after we get settled, and I'm hopeful you will enjoy your life back in Florida.

I love you so much.

Joanie

April 20, 1987

With visibly shaky handwriting, my mother composed this lovely little note on the occasion of my thirty-fifth birthday. She missed the actual date by five days.

Dearest Joanie,

I'm so sorry I forgot your birthday. It just better never happen again. All my love,

Mom

April 27, 1987

Dear Mom,

Today feels different in some way. It's Monday, and I've just wrapped up a long weekend visit with Nancy in Santa Monica, California. Nancy and I have enjoyed a continuous friendship since our days at Baker School. I know how much you adore Nancy. So many times you've referred to her as your "fourth daughter". We chatted, laughed, and shared stories about growing up in Altoona. We also cried with each other, just like sisters.

Flying from Los Angeles to Chicago O'Hare was smooth sailing on this sunny spring day with perfect blue skies. I settled in for the four-hour flight and was fine until we approached our destination.

While on the descent to O'Hare, I suddenly felt very queasy. For the first time ever, I put my head in the barf bag provided by United Airlines in the seat pocket. How bizarre! I've never been sick while flying. Fortunately, for me, and those in my row, I did not progress beyond the nauseated stomach. It was a very strange feeling, but one that passed within fifteen minutes.

It's been four months since we've seen each other. My days have been filled with unpacking our household belongings and arranging the contents in our new space, helping Kristina settle into her new parish school, wrangling Anne each day, and looking for my next teaching assignment. Although we've talked by phone, I still prefer to see you, hug you, and laugh with you in person. I am hoping you have settled into your new apartment with ease.

The flight from Los Angeles to Chicago was quiet today, uneventful, and punctual. All is well in my world, yet something feels different.

More later. . .

Joanie

April 28, 1987

Dear Mom,

You are gone. I feel completely empty inside. On this typical Tuesday evening, while serving a nondescript meal to Kristina and Anne for dinner, the kitchen wall phone rang at precisely 5:20. It was Uncle Squire from Florida, your beloved brother-in-law, and Boonie's husband.

Squire's news hit me like a sledge hammer to the head. I felt pounding in my temples and the accompanying reverberations through my body although I didn't leave the kitchen to collect myself. I continued standing motionless by the wall phone after the conversation ended to let the sorrow sink in completely. Your next-door neighbor found you lying on the carpeted living room floor this afternoon in your Florida apartment. There was no possibility for resuscitation because you had been dead for over twenty- four hours.

While processing this shocking news, I now believe you were in a state of passing in Florida as I was descending to the runway at O'Hare Airport in Chicago yesterday afternoon. With a blue and cloudless sky, no turbulence and a straight path to the designated parking slot for jumbo jets, there was no reason for me to feel sick. Were you also feeling queasy as you passed from this earth a mere twenty-four hours ago?

Is it possible for two people to share the same physical symptoms, although hundreds of miles apart? If so, I *truly* felt your pain yesterday afternoon. This realization confirms why you always described our relationship as *simpatico*. We were one in that moment.

I am devastated, sad, and alone as I write this letter. Even my loving family can't find a way to comfort me today. Your death is my personal life tragedy.

I miss you and love you more than words can express.

Joanie

Mom with Baby Anne
1982

Christmas in Kingwood, Texas
Kristina, Anne, William, James, and Mom
1985

Anne and Mom on Mother's Day
1986

Joanie, Kristina, Anne, and Mom
Christmas in Texas
1986

IN MEMORY OF
Florence Gable Parsons

BORN
October 28, 1924

DATE OF DEATH
April 28, 1987

SERVICE
Robert D. Easter Funeral Chapel
Friday, May 1, 1987
11:00 a.m.

OFFICIATING
Rev. Harry Ferguson

INTERMENT
Woodlawn Memory Gardens

ARRANGEMENTS BY
Robert D. Easter Funeral Home
Gulfport, Florida

God hath not promised
        Skies always blue,
Flower-strewn pathways
        All our lives through;
God hath not promised
        Sun without rain,
Joy without sorrow,
        Peace without pain.

But God hath promised
        Strength for the day,
Rest for the labor,
        Light for the way.
Grace for the trials,
        Help from above,
Unfailing sympathy
        Undying love . . . .

Epilogue

The news of my mother's death in late April of 1987 felt like shock waves through my body. To this day, my heart aches for a woman as lovely, smart, and gracious, as my mother to have drifted to the other side without a hand to hold, without a message of assurance that it would be okay, or without one last whisper telling her how much she meant to me. She died alone in her apartment in Florida.

Since her death, I have carefully absorbed the stories of my friends as they lovingly recounted the final days and hours of their beloved parents' lives. A death story is always filled with lessons for the living. In many cases, the dying seem to be in control of their final months, days, and hours. The lessons from my mother's death included being more aware of a loved one's health and well being. I should have asked questions even if they were uncomfortable. And I had to learn that the dying have their own way of doing things that might not be our way. Honor those desires.

Although my daughters don't ask many questions about my mother and her role as their grandmother, they do acknowledge my closeness to the woman who raised me in Altoona, Pennsylvania, with her values and passions. They understand the kindred spirit that we shared through our love of music, literature, films, card playing at the kitchen table, and pop culture. She was kind to everyone she met, and she could make me laugh like no other person--a hearty belly laugh that always brought tears to my eyes.

Throughout the years, my mother has been a guardian angel to me as she sends positive messages via the words of friends, and even acquaintances. Always delivered with love, these lessons paralleled how she lived her own life. Reviewed and processed during my quietest moments of contemplation, I've mulled over the messages from my mother many times, and they have become invaluable maps on how to navigate the highways of life here on Earth.

Most telling of all messages, my third grandchild, Adeline, presented herself to the world twenty-five years within hours after my mother's passing. This precious baby girl, with her lovely little rosebud lips, blueberry eyes, and blond hair is the living embodiment of all her middle name represents--Hope.

Today, my mission seems clear. The goal is to protect my mother's legacy, to preserve her stories, and to ensure the accuracy of the memories expressed on the preceding pages. For now, I feel confident that the goal is being realized whenever I witness the behavior of my daughters, one with the power to make me laugh until I cry, and the other with my mother's kind heart. With conviction, I can truly say my mother's legacy lives on, her stories live on, and her truth lives on.

Acknowledgments

No project of this magnitude is ever completed without help. First and foremost, I would like to thank my publisher, Shannon Ishizaki, for taking a chance on this book and it's content--for giving the project a heartbeat.

For Denise Guibord Meister, my editor, for understanding the vision of the project from the very beginning, and asking the hard questions throughout the editing process. Thank you.

I cannot forget the many loving friends in my life who have generously shared their own stories of the loss of loved ones and provided me with insight and courage to write about my dear mother. Thank you Jeanne, Cathy, Barbara, Kathy, Mary Lynn, Jan, and Rose.

For the students in my writing class at Lydell School in Whitefish Bay who listened to the stories and provided guidance going forward, especially Gerry, Gordon, Margo, Barbara, and Sally. To our fearless leader, Nancy Martin, who corralled us each week and brought the stories into clearer focus.

To my family, especially Kristina and Anne, the best gifts a mother could ever receive, for their love, encouragement, and support throughout this journey. Even a quick question about the progress of the book was enough to continue the writing. This is for you.

Finally, to Vito, the real encourager throughout the process, who loved my mother as much as I loved her. For knowing how much this story means to me and for providing the gentle nudge to "keep writing." Thank you for the past forty-seven years.

CPSIA information can be obtained
at www.ICGtesting.com
Printed in the USA
LVOW11*1938280317

528799LV00003B/3/P

9 781943 331499